I would like to de[illegible]ok to my master,

Shifu Vineesh.R.P

Without his encouragement
it wasn't possible for me to write this book.

Shifu Vineesh R.P belongs to the 34th generation Shaolin Kung-Fu China, who established Kerala's first genuine Shaolin Temple which was proudly recognized by Songshan Shaolin temple in Henen province(China).

Website : http://www.shaolintemplekerala.in
Contact : +91-9947833975, +91-9526614546
Email : traditionalshaolinkungfu@gmail.com

CONTENTS

INTRODUCTION

Initially I was planning to write a book about martial arts and Buddhism but I was confused that where to begin because there are many systems ,no one can give all the details of these topics in a single book.So I decided to write about Bodhidharma because the more I research about martial arts and Buddhism i realize that through the life and teachings of Bodhidharma I can give a little knowledge about martial arts and Buddhism to my readers.

There are a number of stories and legends surrounding Bodhidharma. Some of that might be real; and a lot others just made up. In any case, they are very interesting. They bring forth the down-to-earth wisdom and the curt wit of Bodhidharma. His life, in many ways, echoes that of the Buddha himself, and his achievements are enormous. Bodhidharma is credited with introducing the form of Buddhism known as Zen to China he is also regarded as the father of Chinese martial arts. There are tens of thousands of Indian and Central Asian monks have journeyed to China by land and sea, but among those who brought the teachings of the Buddha to China, none has had an impact comparable to that of Bodhidharma. Why, then, is he became the most famous of all the millions of monks who have studied and taught the Dharma in China? The reason is that he alone is credited with bringing zen to China. Of course, zen, as meditation, had been taught and practiced for several hundred years before Bodhidharma arrived. And much of what he had to say concerning doctrine had been said before-by Tao-sheng, for example, a hundred years earlier. But Bodhidharma's approach to zen was unique. As he says in these sermons, "Seeing your nature is zen .... Not thinking about anything is zen .... Everything you do is zen." While others viewed zen as purification of the mind or as a stage on the way to buddhahood, Bodhidharma equated zen with buddhahood-and buddhahood with the mind, the everyday mind. Instead of telling his disciples to purify their minds, he pointed them to rock walls, to the movements of tigers and cranes, to a hollow reed floating across the Yangtze, to a single sandal.

Bodhidharma's zen was Mahayana Zen, not Hinayana Zen-the sword of wisdom, not the meditation cushion. As did other masters, he undoubtedly instructed his disciples in Buddhist discipline, meditation, and doctrine, but he used the sword that Prajnatara had given him to cut their minds free from rules, trances, and scriptures. Such a sword, though, is hard to grasp and hard to use. But such a radical understanding of zen didn't originate with Bodhidharma or with Prajnatara. It's said that one day Brahma, lord of creation, offered the Buddha a flower and asked him to preach the Dharma. When the Buddha held up the flower, his audience was puzzled, except for Kashyapa, who smiled. This is how zen began. And this is how it was transmitted: with a flower, with a rock wall, with a shout. This approach, once it was made known by Bodhidharma and his successors, revolutionized the understanding and practice of Buddhism in China. Such an approach doesn't come across very well in books. But in his Further Lives of Exemplary Monks, Tao-hsuan says that Bodhidharma's teachings were written down. Most scholars agree that the Outline of Practice is one such record, but opinion is divided concerning the other three sermons translated here. All three have long been attributed to Bodhidharma, but in recent years a number of scholars have suggested that these sermons are the work of later disciples. There are many texts and many teaching stories which are attributed to Bodhidharma, and yet many of the facts, almost all of the facts of his life and teaching, are lost in history.

1
TYPES OF BUDDHISM

Buddhism arose in northeastern India sometime between the late 6th century and the early 4th century BCE, a period of great social change and intense religious activity. Buddhism, religion and philosophy that developed from the teachings of the Buddha. There is disagreement among scholars about the dates of the Buddha’ s birth and death. Many modern scholars believe that the historical Buddha lived from about 563 to about 483 bce. Many others believe that he lived about 100 years later (from about 448 to 368 bce). At this time in India, there was much discontent with Brahmanic (Hindu high-caste) sacrifice and ritual. In northwestern India there were ascetics who tried to create a more personal and spiritual religious experience than that found in the Vedas (Hindu sacred scriptures). In the literature that grew out of this movement, the Upanishads, a new emphasis on renunciation and transcendental knowledge can be found. Northeastern India, which was less influenced by Vedic tradition, became the breeding ground of many new sects. Society in this area was troubled by the breakdown of tribal unity and the expansion of several petty kingdoms. Religiously, this was a time of doubt, turmoil, and experimentation. A proto-Samkhya group (i.e., one based on the Samkhya school of Hinduism founded by Kapila) was already well established in the area. New sects abounded, including various skeptics (e.g., Sanjaya Belatthiputta), atomists (e.g., Pakudha Kaccayana), materialists (e.g., Ajita Kesakambali), and antinomians (i.e., those against rules or laws—e.g., Purana Kassapa). The most important sects to arise at the time of the Buddha, however, were the Ajivikas (Ajivakas), who emphasized the rule of fate (*niyati*), and the Jains, who stressed the need to free the soul from matter. Although the Jains, like the Buddhists, have often been regarded as atheists, their beliefs are actually more complicated. Unlike early Buddhists, both the Ajivikas and the Jains believed in the permanence of the elements that constitute the universe, as well as in the existence of the soul.

Despite the bewildering variety of religious communities, many shared the same vocabulary—*nirvana* (transcendent freedom), atman ("self" or "soul"), *yoga* ("union"), *karma* ("causality"), *Tathagata* ("one who has come" or "one who has thus gone"), *buddha* ("enlightened one"), *samsara* ("eternal recurrence" or "becoming"), and *dhamma* ("rule" or "law")—and most involved the practice of yoga. According to tradition, the Buddha himself was a yogi—that is, a miracle-working ascetic. Buddhism, like many of the sects that developed in northeastern India at the time, was constituted by the presence of a charismatic teacher, by the teachings this leader promulgated, and by a community of adherents that was often made up of renunciant members and lay supporters. In the case of Buddhism, this pattern is reflected in the Triratna —i.e., the "Three Jewels" of Buddha (the teacher), dharma (the teaching), and sangha (the community). In the centuries following the founder' s death, Buddhism developed in two directions represented by two different groups. One was called the Hinayana (Sanskrit: "Lesser Vehicle"), a term given to it by its Buddhist opponents. This more conservative group, which included what is now called the Theravada (Pali: "Way of the Elders") community, compiled versions of the Buddha' s teachings that had been preserved in collections called the Sutta Pitaka and the Vinaya Pitaka and retained them as normative.

The other major group, which calls itself the Mahayana (Sanskrit: "Greater Vehicle"), recognized the authority of other teachings that, from the group' s point of view, made salvation available to a greater number of people. These supposedly more advanced teachings were expressed in sutras that the Buddha purportedly made available only to his more advanced disciples. As Buddhism spread, it encountered new currents of thought and religion. In some Mahayana communities, for example, the strict law of karma (the belief that virtuous actions create pleasure in the future and nonvirtuous actions create pain) was modified to accommodate new emphases on the efficacy of ritual actions and devotional practices. During the second half of the 1st millennium ce, a third major Buddhist movement, Vajrayana (Sanskrit: "Diamond Vehicle"; also called Tantric, or Esoteric, Buddhism), developed in India. This movement was influenced by gnostic and magical currents pervasive at that time, and its aim was to obtain spiritual liberation and purity more speedily.

Despite these vicissitudes, Buddhism did not abandon its basic principles. Instead, they were reinterpreted, rethought, and reformulated in a process that led to the creation of a great body of literature. This literature includes the Pali Tipitaka ("Three Baskets")—the *Sutta Pitaka* ("Basket of Discourse"), which contains the Buddha' s sermons; the Vinaya Pitaka ("Basket of Discipline"), which contains the rule governing the monastic order; and the Abhidhamma Pitaka ("Basket of Special [Further] Doctrine"), which contains doctrinal systematizations and summaries. These Pali texts have served as the basis for a long and very rich tradition of commentaries that were written and preserved by adherents of the Theravada community. The Mahayana and Vajrayana traditions have accepted as Buddhavachana ("the word of the Buddha") many other sutras and tantras, along with extensive treatises and commentaries based on these texts. Consequently, from the first sermon of the Buddha at Sarnath to the most recent derivations, there is an indisputable continuity—a development or metamorphosis around a central nucleus—by virtue of which Buddhism is differentiated from other religions.

Basically there are 3 major types of Buddhism :

1. Theravada Buddhism .
2. Mahayana Buddhism.
3. Vajrayana Buddhism.

Theravada Buddhism

It is the most ancient branch of Buddhism today. Theravada Buddhism follows the Pali Canon-the oldest recorded teachings of Buddha. Theravada Buddhism emphasises attaining self-liberation through one's own efforts. Meditation and concentration are vital elements of the way to enlightenment. The ideal road is to dedicate oneself to full-time monastic life. The follower is expected to "abstain from all kinds of evil, to accumulate all that is good and to purify their mind". Meditation is one of the main tools by which a Theravada Buddhist transforms themselves, and so a monk spends a great deal of time in meditation. When a person achieves liberation they are called a 'worthy person'

- an *Arhat* or *Arahat*. This can be achieved through meditation, the contemplation of sutras, and following the *Buddha' s Noble Eightfold Path :*

1. **Right vision,**
2. **Right emotion,**
3. **Right speech,**
4. **Right action,**
5. **Right livelihood,**
6. **Right effort,**
7. **Right mindfulness,**
8. **Right meditation.**

Most Theravada monks live as part of monastic communities. Some join as young as seven, but one can join at any age. A novice is called a *samanera* and a full monk is called a *bikkhu.* The monastic community as a whole is called the *sangha*. Monks (and nuns) undertake the training of the monastic order (the Vinaya) which consist of 227 rules (more for nuns). Within these rules or precepts are five which are undertaken by all those trying to adhere to a Buddhist way of life. The Five Precepts are to undertake the rule of training to:

- Refrain from harming living beings
- Refrain from taking that which is not freely given
- Refrain from sexual misconduct
- Refrain from wrong speech; such as lying, idle chatter, malicious gossip or harsh speech
- Refrain from intoxicating drink and drugs which lead to carelessness

Of particular interest is the fact that Theravadan monks and nuns are not permitted to eat after midday or handle money.

Theravada beliefs :

- ❖ The Supernatural: Many faiths offer supernatural solutions to the spiritual problems of human beings. Buddhism does not. The basis of all forms of Buddhism is to use meditation for awakening (or enlightenment), not outside powers.

- Supernatural powers are not disregarded but they are incidental and the Buddha warned against them as fetters on the path.

- The Buddha: Siddhartha Gautama was a man who became Buddha, the Awakened One - much in the same way as Jesus became Christ. Since his death the only contact with him is through his teachings which point to the awakened state.
- God: There is no omnipotent creator God of the sort found in Judaism, Islam and Christianity. Gods exist as various types of spiritual being but with limited powers.
- The Path to Enlightenment: Each being has to make their own way to enlightenment without the help of God or gods. Buddha's teachings show the way, but making the journey is up to us.

Today, Theravada Buddhism is most popular in Sri Lanka, Thailand, Laos, Cambodia, and Myanmar.

Mahayana Buddhism

Mahayana Buddhism is strongest in Tibet, China, Taiwan, Japan, Korea, and Mongolia. Mahayana Buddhism is not a single group but a collection of Buddhist traditions: Zen Buddhism, Pure Land Buddhism, and Tibetan Buddhism are all forms of Mahayana Buddhism. The precise origin of Mahayana Buddhism is unknown. It appeared sometime between 150 BC and AD 100 in India and quickly spread throughout Asia. It came about with the introduction of new sutras, or authoritative teachings of the Buddha.Like Theraveda Buddhism, Mahayana is both a philosophy and a way of life that aspires to nirvana. Nirvana is a state of enlightenment that comes with the recognition that the ego, or the thing we think of as our self, is an illusion that causes us pain and suffering.

Theravada and Mahayana are both rooted in the basic teachings of the historical Buddha, and both emphasise the individual search for liberation from the cycle of *samsara* (birth, death, rebirth...). The methods or practices for doing that, however, can be very different. Mahayana differs from the Theraveda tradition in three basic ways :

1. Mahayan emphasizes sunyata, or the emptiness that comes with enlightenment. While Theravada Buddhism suggests that sunyata is the ultimate basis of all things, Mahayana holds that no such basis exists, that nothing is anything until compared to something else. Put briefly, everything is nothing! Mahayana embraces the letting go of all phenomena as aspects of illusion.
2. Mahayana also differs in its preferred path to enlightenment. The Mahayana tradition privileges the Bodhisattva-path. A bodhisattva is one who has achieved enlightenment but postpones full nirvana to help others on their paths to do the same. Unlike the Theravada tradition, which held that enlightenment required years of careful study by trained monks and sometimes required multiple reincarnated lifetimes to achieve, Mahayana tradition holds that any individual can take up the bodhisattva-path and that enlightenment can occur suddenly and within one lifetime.
3. Mahayana Buddhism celebrates the Buddha as transcendent being and encourages the use of his image, as a meditative tool or object of devotion. Depictions of heroic bodhisattvas are also associated with Mahayana Buddhism.

Mahayana talks a great deal about the bodhisattva (the 'enlightenment being') as being the ideal way for a Buddhist to live. Anyone can embark on the bodhisattva path. This is a way of life, a way of selflessness; it is a deep wish for all beings, no matter who they are, to be liberated from suffering.

The Boddhisattva Vow :

- ❖ However innumerable sentient beings are, I vow to save them.
- ❖ However inexhaustible the defilements are, I vow to extinguish them.
- ❖ However immeasurable the dharmas are, I vow to master them.
- ❖ However incomparable enlightenment is, I vow to attain it.

Mahayana Buddhism says that there are three aspects of Buddhahood, which it describes by regarding Buddha as having three bodies (trikaya) :

- *Dharmakaya*: Buddha is transcendent - he is the same thing as the ultimate truth.
- *Sambhogakaya*: Buddha's body of bliss, or enjoyment body.
- *Nirmanakaya*: Buddha's earthly body - just like any other human being's body.

Mahayana Buddhism greater emphasis on mantras, chanting, especially in Tibetan Buddhism.Though Tibetan Buddhism is based on Mahayana, it could be seen as its own strand – Vajrayana. Tibetan Buddhism is based on Tantric disciplines.

Vajrayana Buddhism

Vajrayana Buddhism, also known as the "Diamond" or "Thunderbolt Vehicle," is a form of Buddhism that developed in India in the 5th century C.E. Although it is sometimes debated whether it is a branch of Mahayana Buddhism or if it is a distinct path beside Mahayana and Theravada—this is how the tradition understands itself, as the final "turning" of the Buddha's teachings—it is generally accepted that Vajrayana Buddhism emerged out of the Mahayana in India, probably in the 6th-7th centuries. According to some ancient tradition, *Vajrayana* is understood as the final turning of Buddha teachings . *Vajrayana Buddhism* is given many names such as Tantric Buddhism, Tantrayana, Mantrayana, Esoteric Buddhism and sometimes Tibetan Buddhism . It is believed in *Vajrayana Buddhism* that the Lama and the Guru Yoga are central aspects in *Vajrayana* . Though *Vajrayana* evolved from *Mahayana* and *Theravada Buddhism* , it became one of the dominant *Buddhist practice* and spread quite rapidly in India, and Tibet in the 6-7th Centuries. The highest goal of *Vajrayana Buddhism* is to become the Bodhisattva . Experiencing this highest goal and ultimate truth is the main purpose of all tantric techniques which are practiced in *Vajrayana Buddhism.* Motivation is one of the main components of *Vajrayana* tradition. The *Bodhisattva* path practiced in *Vajrayana* is the integral part which teaches that the practices should be done with the motivation to achieve ultimate truth, Buddhahood and should be used for the sake helping all the sentient beings to end suffering and pain.

2
LIFE OF BUDDHA

Before we go furthur into the life of bodhidharma and his teachings we should know the life of Budha. Buddhism is an important religion in most of the countries of Asia and is the world' s fourth largest religion with over 520 million followers, or over 7% of the global population.Buddhism, founded in the late 6th century B.C.E. by Siddhartha Gautama (the "Buddha"). The history of Buddhism is also characterized by the development of numerous movements, schisms, and schools, among them the Theravāda, Mahāyāna and Vajrayāna traditions, with contrasting periods of expansion and retreat. However all the branches of Buddhism is based on the life and teachings of Buddha.So before learn about Buddhism one should know about the life of Buddha.

Many valuable books have been written by Eastern and Western scholars, Buddhists and non-Buddhists alike, to present the life and teachings of the Buddha to those who are interested in Buddhism. However, not until the writing of the Buddha Charita (life of the Buddha) by Ashvaghosa in the 1st or 2nd century C.E. do we have acomprehensive account of his life. Siddhartha Gautama, was born in the Sixth century BCE in Lumbini,what is now nepal, to the north of the holy Indian city of Varanasi. His father Suddhodana was King of the Shakya clan, ruler of one of several kingdoms that existed in India and Nepal at the time. It said that he was mastered all kind of art and science without needing any instruction.He knows 64 different languages. He was a skilled martial artist too. At one time, when he was taking part in an archery contest, he declared, "With the bow of meditative concentration I will fire the arrow of wisdom and kill the tiger of ignorance in living beings." He then released the arrow and it flew straight through five iron tigers and seven trees before disappearing into the earth! According to legend, at his birth a soothsayer predicted that he might become a renouncer (withdrawing from the temporal life). To prevent this, his father provided him with many luxuries and pleasures.

The path to his enlightenment begins when he go into the capital city of his father's kingdom to see how the people lived. During these visits he came into contact with many old people and sick people The contrast between his life and this human suffering made him realize that all living beings without exception have to experience the sufferings of birth, sickness, ageing and death. So he wish to free all of them from their suffering but he realize that only the enlightened one have the power to help others from this suffering. So he leave his royal life and go into a forest and he engage in meditation.He traveled to Bodh Gaya, in India where he found a suitable site for meditation. There he remained, emphasizing a meditation called "space-like concentration on the Dharmakaya" in which he focused single-pointedly on the ultimate nature of all phenomena. After training in this meditation for six years he realized that he was very close to attaining full enlightenment, and so he walked to Bodh Gaya where, on the full moon day of the fourth month of the lunar calendar, he seated himself beneath the Bodhi Tree in the meditation posture and vowed not to rise from meditation until he had attained perfect enlightenment. With this determination he entered the space-like concentration on the Dharmakaya.With this concentration, which is the very last mind of a limited being, he removed the final veils of ignorance from his mind and in the next moment became a Buddha, a fully enlightened being.

FORMATION OF THE SANGHA

After his awakening Buddha met two merchants brothers Taphussa and Bhallika who became his first disciples. They are given some hairs from the Buddha's head, which are believed to now be enshrined in the Shwe Dagon Temple in Rangoon, Burma. The Buddha intended to visit Asita, and his former teachers, Alara Kalama and Uddaka Ramaputta to explain his findings, but they had already died. He then travelled to Deer Park near Vārāṇasī (Benares) in northern India, where he set in motion call the Wheel of Dharma by delivering his first sermon to the five companions with whom he had sought enlightenment. Together with him, they formed the first Sangha : the company of Buddhist monks and hence, the first formation of Triple Gem (Buddha, Dharma and Sangha) was completed, with Kaundinya becoming the first stream-enterer. For the remaining he was travel all around the India and Nepal and spread his teachings.All five become arahants, and within the first two months, with the conversion of Yasa and fifty-four of his friends, the number of such arahants is said to have grown to 60. The conversion of three brothers named Kassapa followed, with their reputed 200, 300 and 500 disciples, respectively. This swelled the sangha to more than 1,000.

It is unknown what language the Buddha spoke, and no conclusive documentation has been made at this point. However, some modern scholars, primarily philologists, believe it is most likely that the Buddha spoke a vulgate then current in eastern India, Mâgadhî Prakrit. Magadhi Prakrit is the spoken language of the ancient Magadha kingdom, one of the 16 city-state kingdoms at the time, located in the eastern Indian subcontinent, in a region around modern-day Bihār, and spanning what is now eastern India, Bangladesh, and Nepal. The first Magadha king is Bimbisara (558 BC –491 BC), during whose reign the Buddha attained enlightenment. Both king Bimbisara and his successor son Ajatashatru, were mentioned in several Buddhist Sutras, being lay disciplines, great friends and protectors of the Buddha.

MAHAPARINIRVANA (DEATH)

In order to know the last day of the Buddha, we should read books on his life or better still, read the recorded suttas. Scholars say that the best source is the Maha Parinibbana Sutta from the Pali collection of the Digha Nikaya, or the Wandering Sutra from the Sanskrit/Chinese collection of the Digha Agama. There is a separate Chinese sutra, The Maha Parinirvana Sutra, which was also translated into Vietnamese, but this script has been widely regarded as being composed at a very late stage. According to the *Mahaparinibbana Sutta* of the Pali canon, at the age of 80 he reach parinirvana or the final deathless state.He inform his followers about leaving his earthly body. It is to be said that he ate his last meal from a blacksmith named Cunda falling violently ill Buddha instructed his attendant Ananda to convince Cunda that the meal eaten at his place had nothing to do with his passing and that his meal would be a source of the greatest merit as it provided the last meal for a Buddha. After his death, Buddha's cremation relics were divided amongst 8 royal families and his disciples; centuries later they would be enshrined by King Ashoka into 84,000 stupas. Many supernatural legends surround the history of alleged relics as they accompanied the spread of Buddhism and gave legitimacy to rulers. The Buddha's final words are reported to have been: "All composite things (Saṅkhā ra) are perishable. Strive for your own liberation with diligence"

3
MASTER OF ZEN

Bodhidharma was a Buddhist monk who lived during the 5th/6th century and is traditionally credited as the leading patriarch and transmitter of Zen to China. Little contemporary biographical information on Bodhidharma is extant, and subsequent accounts became layered with legend, but some accounts state that he was from a Brahman family in southern India and possibly of royal lineage.However Broughton (1999:2) notes that Bodhidharma's royal pedigree implies that he was of the Kshatriya warrior caste. Mahajan (1972:705 – 707) argued that the Pallava dynasty was a Tamilian dynasty and Zvelebil (1987)

proposed that Bodhidharma was born a prince of the Pallava dynasty in their capital of Kanchipuram Scholars have concluded his place of birth to be Kanchipuram in Tamil Nadu, India. The youngest of three brothers, Bodhidharma was trained in breathing exercises as he was born with a breathing disorder. He was also trained in Dravidian warfare and self-defense techniques. However, martial arts historians have shown this legend stems from a 17th century qigong manual known as the Yijin Jing. Throughout Buddhist art, Bodhidharma is depicted as a rather ill-tempered, profusely bearded and wide-eyed barbarian. He is described as "The Blue-Eyed Barbarian" in Chinese texts. The Anthology of the Patriarchal Hall (952) identifies Bodhidharma as the 28th Patriarch of Buddhism in an uninterrupted line that extends all the way back to the Buddha himself. D.T. Suzuki contends that Chán's growth in popularity during the 7th and 8th centuries attracted criticism that it had "no authorized records of its direct transmission from the founder of Buddhism" and that Chán historians made Bodhidharma the 28th patriarch of Buddhism in response to such attacks.

In the midst of his education and training to continue in his father's footsteps as king, Bodhidharma encountered the Buddha's teachings. He immediately saw the truth in Lord Buddha's words and decided to give up his esteemed position and inheritance to study with the famous Buddhist teacher Prajnatara. Bodhidharma rapidly progressed in his Buddhist studies, Bodhidharma studied Dhyana Buddhism and became the 28th patriarch of this religion. At the age of 22, Bodhidharma attained enlightenment and in time, Prajnatara sent Bodhidharma to China, where Buddhism had begun to die out, to introduce the Sarvastivada sect Buddhist teachings to the Chinese. Bodhidharma arrived in China after a brutal trek over Tibet's Himalayan Mountains surviving both the extreme elements and treacherous bandits.
The accounts differ on the date of his arrival, with one early account claiming that he arrived during the Liú Sòng Dynasty (420–479) and later accounts dating his arrival to the Liáng Dynasty (502–557). Bodhidharma was primarily active in the lands of the Northern Wèi Dynasty (386–534). Bodhidharma crossed through Guangdong province and entered China while he was practising Da Sheng (Mahayana) Buddhism and was known as Da Mo. He was greeted by a large crowd who had heard about the famous Buddhist master and wanted to hear him speak. But he sat down to meditate for many hours.

After completing his meditation, Bodhidharma rose and walked away without saying a word. This action of his had a profound effect on the crowd and this incident made Bodhidharma even more famous. so famous that Emperor Wu heard of him. Emperor Wu ruled the southern kingdom of China and invited Bodhidharma to his palace. The emperor talked to Bodhidharma about Buddhism. The emperor was hoping to receive praise from Bodhidharma but his negative response enraged Wu who ordered Bodhidharma to leave and never return. Da Mo continued his journey, heading north, when he reached the city of Nanjing. In the city of Nanjing, there was a famous place called the Flower Rain Pavillion where many people gathered to speak and relax. There was a large crowd of people gathered in the Flower Rain Pavillion around a Buddhist monk, who was lecturing. This Buddhist monk was named Shen Guang. Shen Guang had at one time been a famous general. He had killed many people in battle but one day realized that the people he had been killing had family and friends and that one day someone might come and kill him. This changed him and he decided to train as a Buddhist monk. Eventually, Shen Guang became a great speaker on Buddhism. As Da Mo neared the crowd, he listened to Shen Guang's speech. Sometimes Shen Guang would speak and Da Mo would nod his head, as if in agreement. Sometimes Shen Guang would speak and Da Mo would shake his head, as if in disagreement. As this continued, Shen Guang became very angry at the strange foreign monk who dared to disagree with him in front of this crowd. In anger, Shen Guang took the Buddhist beads from around his neck and flicked them at Da Mo. The beads struck Da Mo in his face, knocking out two of his front teeth. Da Mo immediately began bleeding. Shen Guang expected a confrontation; instead, Da Mo smiled, turned and walked away. This reaction astounded Shen Guang, who began following after Da Mo. Da Mo continued north until he reached the Yangzi river. Seated by the river there was an old woman with a large bundle of reeds next to her. Da Mo walked up to the old woman and asked her if he might have a reed. She replied that he might. Da Mo took a single reed, placed it upon the surface of the Yangzi river and stepped onto the reed. He was carried across the Yangzi river by the force of his chi. Seeing this, Shen Guang ran up to where the old woman sat and grabbed a handful of reeds without asking. He threw the reeds onto the Yangzi river and stepped onto them. The reeds sank beneath him and Shen Guang began drowning. The old woman saw his plight and took pity on Shen Guang, pulling him from the river. As Shen Guang lay on the ground coughing up river water, the old woman admonished him. She said that by not asking for her reeds before taking them, he had shown her disrespect and that by disrespecting her, Shen Guang had disrespected himself. The old woman also told Shen Guang that he had been searching for a master and that Da Mo, the man he was following, was that master. As she said this, the reeds which had sunk beneath Shen Guang rose again to the surface of the river and Shen Guang found himself on the reeds being carried across the Yangzi river. He reached the other side and continued following after Da Mo. There are many people who believe that the old woman by the river was a Boddhisatva who was helping Shen Guang to end the cycle of his samsara. At this point, Da Mo was nearing the location of the Shaolin Temple. The Shaolin monks had heard of his approach and were gathered to meet him. When Da Mo arrived, the Shaolin monks greeted him and invited him to come stay at the temple. Da Mo did not reply but he went to a cave on a mountain behind the Shaolin Temple, sat down, and began meditating. In front of the Shaolin Temple, there are five mountains: Bell Mountain, Drum Mountain, Sword Mountain, Stamp Mountain and Flag Mountain. These mountains are named after the objects which their shape resembles. Behind the Shaolin Temple there are five "Breast Mountains" which are shaped like breasts. The cave in which Da Mo chose to meditate was on one of the Breast Mountains. Da Mo sat facing a wall in the cave and meditated for nine years. During these nine years, Shen Guang stayed outside Da Mo's cave and acted as a bodyguard for Da Mo, ensuring that no harm came to Da Mo. Periodically Shen Guang would ask Da Mo to teach him, but Da Mo never responded to Shen Guang's requests. During these nine years the Shaolin monks would also periodically invite Da Mo to come down to the Temple, where he would be much more comfortable, but Da Mo never responded. After some time, Da Mo's concentration became so intense that his image was engraved into the stone of the wall before him.

Towards the end of the nine years, the Shaolin monks decided that they must do something more for Da Mo and so they made a special room for him. They called this room the Da Mo Ting. When this room was completed at the end of the nine years, the Shaolin monks invited Da Mo to come stay in the room. Da Mo did not respond but he stood up, walked down to the room, sat down, and immediately began meditating. Shen Guang followed Da Mo to the Shaolin temple and stood guard outside Da Mo's room. Da Mo meditated in his room for another four years. Shen Guang would occasionally ask Da Mo to teach him, but Da Mo never responded. At the end of the four-year period Shen Guang had been following Da Mo for thirteen years, but Da Mo had never said anything to Shen Guang. It was winter when the four-year period was ending and Shen Guang was standing in the snow outside the window to Da Mo' s room. He was cold and became very angry. He picked up a large block of snow and ice and hurled it into Da Mo' s room. The snow and ice made a loud noise as it broke inside Da Mo' s room. This noise awoke Da Mo from his meditation and he looked at Shen Guang. In anger and frustration Shen Guang demanded to know when Da Mo would teach him. Da Mo responded that he would teach Shen Guang when red snow fell from the sky. Hearing this, something inside Shen Guang' s heart changed and he took the sword he carried from his belt and cut off his left arm. He held the severed arm above his head and whirled it around. The blood from the arm froze in the cold air and fell like red snow. Seeing this, Da Mo agreed to teach Shen Guang.

Da Mo took a monk' s spade and went with Shen Guang to the Drum Mountain in front of Shaolin Temple. The Drum Mountain is so called because it is very flat on top. Da Mo' s unspoken message to Shen Guang was that Shen Guang should flatten his heart, just like the surface of the Drum Mountain. On this Drum Mountain Da Mo dug a well. The water of this well was bitter. Da Mo then left Shen Guang on the Drum Mountain. For an entire year, Shen Guang used the bitter water of the well to take care of all of his needs. He used it to cook, to clean, to bathe, to do everything. At the end of the first year, Shen Guang went down to Da Mo and again asked Da Mo to teach him. Da Mo returned with Shen Guang to the Drum Mountain and dug a second well. The water of this well was spicy. For an entire year, Shen Guang used the spicy water for all of his needs. At the end of the second year, Shen Guang went back down to Da Mo and asked again to be taught. Da Mo dug a third well on the Drum Mountain. The water of this third well was sour. For the third year, Shen Guang used the sour water for all of his needs. At the end of the third year, Shen Guang returned to Da Mo and agains asked to be taught. Da Mo returned to the Drum Mountain and dug a fourth and final well. The water of this well was sweet. At this point, Shen Guang realized that the four wells represented his life. Like the wells, his life would sometimes be bitter, sometimes sour, sometimes spicy and sometimes sweet. Each of these phases in his life was equally beautiful and necessary, just as each of the four seasons of the year is beautiful and necessary in its own way. Without really saying many words to Shen Guang, Da Mo had taught Shen Guang the most important of lessons in a mind-to-mind, heart-to-heart fashion. This mind-to- mind, heart-to-heart communication is called "action language" and is the foundation of the Chan Buddhism which Da Mo began at the Shaolin Temple. After his realization, Shen Guang was given the name Hui Ke and he became abbot of the Shaolin temple after Da Mo. To pay respect for the sacrifice which Hui Ke made, disciples and monks of the Shaolin Temple greet each other using only their right hand.

Bodhidharma was not a prolific writer or philosopher like other Buddhist figures, yet the central elements of his teachings can be seen in stories of his life such as his emphasis on *zazen*, his style of interacting with students (often referred to as "dharma-dueling" and found in many *koan*s), the lack of emphasis on scholarship and intellectual debate, and the importance of personal realization and mind-to-mind transmission from teacher to disciple. These distinctive features that Bodhidharma brought from India to China almost 1,500 years ago still define Zen Buddhism today. Tradition holds that Bodhidharma's principal text was the Lankavatara Sutra, a development of the *Yogacara* or "Mind-only" school of Buddhism established by the Gandharan half-brothers Asanga and Vasubandhu. He is described as a "master of the Lankavatara Sutra," and an early history of Zen in China is titled *Record of the Masters and Disciples of the Lankavatara Sutra* (Chinese, *Leng-ch'ieh shih-tzu chi*). Some sources go so far as to credit Bodhidharma with being the first to introduce this sutra to China. This emphasis on the *Yogacara* philosophy of "Mind-only" is often expressed in his discourses:

"Your mind is nirvana, you might think that you can find a Buddha or enlightenment somewhere beyond the mind, but such a place does not exist."

He also lectured extensively on the doctrine of emptiness (*shunyata*), a defining feature of Mahayana thought found in the Prajnaparamita Sutras and the writings of Nagarjuna (c. 150-250) and his school of Madhyamaka. In one example, he states that "the sutras tell us... to see without seeing... to hear without hearing, to know without knowing... Basically, seeing, hearing, and knowing are completely empty" (Red Pine 1987, 27). This passage expresses another distinct feature of Zen: we should act without conceptualization or (as a result) hesitation. All things and all actions are held to be "empty" of any intellectual elaborations, and exist freely and spontaneously as direct expressions of nothing other than themselves. This influence is seen in Zen's insistence on natural and immediate actions and responses, as seen in numerous *koans*, interactions between teachers and students, and in Zen art. One common example of this is a student shouting in response to a teacher's question as a way of demonstrating their understanding. If the student is able to do so without hesitation and with their whole being, then they are said to have shown their master their 'Zen Mind.' Another characteristic feature of Bodhidharma' s presentation of Buddhism was the emphasis he placed on physical well-being. He taught that keeping our bodies healthy increases our mental energy and prepares us for the rigors that serious meditation practice requires. Bodhidharma's mind-and-body approach to spiritual practice ultimately proved highly attractive to the Samurai class in Japan, who incorporated Zen into their way of life, following their encounter with the martial-arts-oriented Zen Rinzai School introduced to Japan by Eisai in the twelfth century. The cause and age of his death are unclear. One story recounts how two teachers, jealous of his renown, tried to poison him on several occasions. After their sixth attempt, he decided that, having successfully spread his teaching to China, it was time for him to pass into parinirvana. He is said to have died soon after sitting in *zazen*.

The *Anthology of the Patriarchal Hall* states that Bodhidharma died at the age of 150. He was then buried on Mount Xiong'er (*Xióng'ěr Shān*) to the west of Luoyang. However, three years after the burial, in the Pamir Mountains, Sòngyún an official of one of the later Wei kingdoms—encountered Bodhidharma, who claimed to be returning to India and was carrying a single sandal. Bodhidharma predicted the death of Songyun's ruler, a prediction which was borne out upon the latter's return. Bodhidharma's tomb was then opened, and only a single sandal was found inside.

23

Three years after Bodhidharma's death, Ambassador Sòngyún of northern Wei is said to have seen him walking while holding a shoe at the Pamir Heights. Sòngyún asked Bodhidharma where he was going, to which Bodhidharma replied "I am going home". When asked why he was holding his shoe, Bodhidharma answered "You will know when you reach Shaolin monastery. Don't mention that you saw me or you will meet with disaster". After arriving at the palace, Sòngyún told the emperor that he met Bodhidharma on the way. The emperor said Bodhidharma was already dead and buried and had Sòngyún arrested for lying. At Shaolin Monastery, the monks informed them that Bodhidharma was dead and had been buried in a hill behind the temple. The grave was exhumed and was found to contain a single shoe. The monks then said "Master has gone back home" and prostrated three times: "For nine years he had remained and nobody knew him; Carrying a shoe in hand he went home quietly, without ceremony."

4
ZEN BUDDHISM

Zen, Chinese **Chan**, Korean **Sŏn**, also spelled **Seon**, Vietnamese **Thien**, important school of East Asian Buddhism that constitutes the mainstream monastic form of Mahayana Buddhism in China, Korea, and Vietnam and accounts for approximately 20 percent of the Buddhist temples in Japan. The word derives from the Sanskrit *dhyana*, meaning "meditation." Central to Zen teaching is the belief that awakening can be achieved by anyone but requires instruction in the proper forms of spiritual cultivation by a master. In modern times, Zen has been identified especially with the secular arts of medieval Japan (such as the tea ceremony, ink painting, and gardening) and with any spontaneous expression of artistic or spiritual vitality regardless of context. In popular usage, the modern non-Buddhist connotations of the word Zen have become so prominent that in many cases the term is used as a label for phenomena that lack any relationship to Zen or are even antithetical to its teachings and practices.

Compiled by the Chinese Buddhist monk Daoyun in 1004, *Records of the Transmission of the Lamp* (*Chingde chongdeng lu*) offers an authoritative introduction to the origins and nature of Zen Buddhism. The work describes the Zen school as consisting of the authentic Buddhism practiced by monks and nuns who belong to a large religious family with five main branches, each branch of which demonstrates its legitimacy by performing Confucian-style ancestor rites for its spiritual ancestors or patriarchs. The genealogical tree of this spiritual lineage begins with the seven buddhas, consisting of six mythological Buddhas of previous eons as well as Siddhartha Gautama, or Shakyamuni, the historical Buddha of the current age. The spiritual awakening and wisdom realized by these buddhas then was transmitted from master to disciple across 28 generations of semi-historical or mythological Buddhist teachers in India, concluding with Bodhidharma, the monk who supposedly introduced true Buddhism to China in the 5th century. This true Buddhism held that its practitioners could achieve a sudden awakening to spiritual truth, which they could not accomplish by a mere reading of Buddhist scriptures. As Bodhidharma asserted in a verse attributed to him Zen began to emerge as a distinctive school of Mahayana Buddhism when Bodhidharma (ca. 470–543) transported Dhyan at the Shaolin Monastery of China. This Chan went further down to Indonesia, Japan, and other far east Asian countries, where it became Zen. Zen's golden age began with the Sixth Patriarch, Hui-neng (638-713), and ended with the persecution of Buddhism in China in the middle of the 9th century CE. Most of those we think of today as the great Zen masters came from this period. Zen Buddhism survived the persecution though it was never the same again in China. Zen spread to Korea in the 7th century CE and to Japan in the 12th century CE. It was popularised in the West by the Japanese scholar Daisetz Teitaro Suzuki (1870 - 1966); although it was found in the West before that. From the time of Bodhidharma to the present, each generation of the Zen lineage claimed to have attained the same spiritual awakening as its predecessors, thereby preserving the Buddha' s "lamp of wisdom." This genealogical ethos confers religious authority on present-day Zen teachers as the legitimate heirs and living representatives of all previous Buddhas and patriarchs. It also provides the context of belief for various Zen rituals, such as funeral services performed by Zen priests and ancestral memorial rites for the families of laypeople who patronize the temples. The Zen ethos that people in each new generation can and must attain spiritual awakening does not imply any rejection of thé usual forms of Buddhist spiritual cultivation, such as the study of scriptures, the performance of good deeds, and the practice of rites and ceremonies, image worship, and ritualized forms of meditation.

Zen teachers typically assert rather that all of these practices must be performed correctly as authentic expressions of awakening, as exemplified by previous generations of Zen teachers. For this reason, the *Records of the Transmission of the Lamp* attributes the development of the standard format and liturgy of the Chinese Buddhist monastic institution to early Zen patriarchs, even though there is no historical evidence to support this claim. Beginning at the time of the Song dynasty (960–1279), Chinese monks composed strict regulations to govern behaviour at all publicly recognized Buddhist monasteries. Known as "rules of purity" (Chinese: *qinggui*, Japanese: *shingi*), these rules were frequently seen as unique expressions of Chinese Zen. In fact, however, the monks largely codified traditional Buddhist priestly norms of behaviour, and, at least in China, the rules were applied to residents of all authorized monasteries, whether affiliated with the Zen school or not. Zen monks and nuns typically study Buddhist scriptures, Chinese classics, poetics, and Zen literature. Special emphasis traditionally has been placed on the study of "public cases" (Chinese: *gongan*; Japanese: *kōan*), or accounts of episodes in which Zen patriarchs reportedly attained awakening or expressed their awakening in novel and iconoclastic ways, using enigmatic language or gestures. Included in the *Records of the Transmission of the Lamp* and in other hagiographic compendia, the public cases are likened to legal precedents that are designed to guide the followers of Zen.

Zen practices are aimed at taking the rational and intellectual mind out of the mental loop, so that the students of Zen aim to achieve enlightenment by the way they live, and by mental actions that approach the truth without philosophical thought or intellectual endeavour.what is really the essence of Zen Buddhism? One has to understand that Zen Buddhism is not a theory, or a body of knowledge. It is not a belief, a canon, or a religion; but rather, it is a practical experience. Zen is not something you can intellectualize, it is your personal experience of the here and the now. Zen does not worry about the afterlife, reincarnation, or God, it is focused on this moment - right now. Moreover, Zen accepts that a human being is a mere mortal who is incapable of answering the universe' s impossible questions. If we look deep into the Zen teachings especially the Zen meditation we can see that it developed from the Indian yoga. The Ashtanga Yoga said that you have to go through 8 steps to attain "Samadhi" the state which you became one with the divine.The steps are :

1. Yamam.
2. Niyamam.
3. Asanam.
4. Pranayamam.
5. Prethyaharam.
6. Dharana.
7. Dhynam.
8. Samadhi.

As we know Zen Buddhism is a branch of Mahayana Buddhism so the Zen created by the Buddhist teachings combine with the Indian Yoga.If you learn Buddhism and yoga together you can understand this. For example The sitting postures in Zen meditation is actually taken from the Yoga.

Cross legged position (Padmasana)

Vajrasana

And the zen meditation is the combination of Prethyaharam (Look into oneself) and Dharana (fix your mind in a certain thing). at the beginning of the training Zen practitioners try to avoid all kind of outside distractions and see oneself like a mirror its called Prethyahara then they train to not think of anything and fix your mind in nothingness thats called Dharana in Yoga.So it is sure that Indian yoga has great impact on Zen Buddhism.

ZEN MEDITATION

At the core of Zen Buddhism is Zen meditation or Zazen, meaning sitting. It is basically seated meditation wherein the one practicing it is in good posture, "pushing the sky" with the top of his head, paying careful attention to breathing, until he is fully alert and present. The end goal of Zen Buddhism is to take someone' s rational and intellectual mind out of the mental loop, so that he can realize his own Buddha-nature.

The practice of Zen meditation or Zazen is at the heart of the Zen Buddhist experience. Originally called Dhyana in India, Zen meditation is a very simple yet precise method of meditation, where the correct posture is imperative.The detailes given below :-

1. Find a quiet and peaceful place where you will not be disturbed. The room where you will practice in should not be too dark or too bright, too warm or too cold.
2. Sit in lotus position.postures might seem uncomfortable and unnatural for most beginners, but with practice, your legs and hips will become more flexible, your mind will relax, and you will find the posture to be quite comfortable.If the posture is too uncomfortable, try sitting in seiza, the traditional kneeling position used in Japan(and called Vajrasana in yoga) for regular sitting in daily life.Keep your neck straight as possible and your tongue should be against the roof of your mouth just behind our teeth and traditionally the eyes kept open during the meditation Without focusing on nothing in particular, direct your vision about one meter in front of you on the floor. Your eyes will naturally come to rest in a position that is half opened and half closed. The position of the hands during Zazen is called cosmic mudra.First, put your left hand on the right one, and palms turned

towards the sky. Now, make an oval by touching the tips of the thumbs together so that your thumbs touch each other and form a somewhat straight line. The tips of your thumbs should lightly touch each other. Both of your wrists should rest on your thighs; the edge of your hands should rest against your belly. Keep your shoulders relaxed.

3. Breathing is a is a fundamental part of the Zazen practice.Your breath should be deep long and natural.and concentrate on the breathing.As with breathing, the mindset is essential in the practice of Ze meditation. The right state of mind emerges naturally from a deep concentration on the posture and breathing. During zazen, it is normal to have images, thoughts and emotions coming up to the surface, appearing from the unconscious mind. Do not pursue them or fight escape from them. The more you try to get rid of them, the more a ttention you give them, and the stronger they become. Try not to attach to them. Just let them go without judgement, like clouds in the sky.So, as soon as you become aware that you are interacting or grasping on thoughts, immediately bring back your concentration to your posture and breathing; your mind will settle down naturally.With experience, you will have less and less thoughts during Zazen, and your mind will come to rest more easily and more quickly.

4. Now it' s time to start Zazen. To avoid distraction, it is recommended that you practice facing a wall, as you would do in a training hall (dojo) or a monastery. Place your zafu on your zabuton so that, once sitting, your body is about one meter away from the wall. If you are using a kneeling bench or a chair, also try to position yourself a meter away from the wall.Once you have finished Zazen, do gassho again. Remain sitting on the cushion calmly and quietly for a few moments; don't hurry to stand up. Try not to talk for a few minutes after completing Zazen.

5
SHAOLIN KUNG FU

Shaolin Kung Fu is the one of the oldest martial arts after Kalaripayattu and it is the lagest and most famous styles of Wushu or Kung Fu. Shaolin Kung Fu combines Zen Buddhism and Martial arts together. Many people are under the impression that Kung Fu originated with the Shaolin Temple. It did not. Chinese martial arts were well developed before the Shaolin Temple was built. The temple was built in the third century A.D, but there are references to such individuals as the physician Hwa Tuo who was using exercises based on animal movements to improve the physical health of his patients well before that date. Hwa Tuo lived at the time of the Three Kingdom, around A.D. 220-65. Hwa Tuo is said to have created a set of exercises based upon five animals: the tiger, bear, monkey, stork and dear. The reason this is significant is that there is even today a strong relationship between animal movement and the Chinese martial arts.

Thirty years after Shaolin was founded, Bodhidharma came to China to teach Zen Buddhism. He traveled throughout China and finally came to Mt. Song where he found Shaolin Temple where he asked to be admitted. The abbot, Fang Chang, refused, and it is said Bodhidharma climbed high into the mountains to a cave where he meditated for nine years. It is believed that he sat, facing the cave wall for much of these nine years so that his shadow became permanently outlined on the cave wall. (Incidentally, the cave is now a sacred place and the shadow imprint has been removed from the cave and moved to the temple compound where you can view it during your visit. It is quite remarkable.) After nine years, Fang Chang finally granted Bodhidharma entrance to Shaolin where he became the First Patriarch of Zen Buddhism. When he entered Shaolin Temple found that the monks there were not very fit. He introduced a series of exercises to them through two books, the *Yin Gin Ching* and the *Shi Sui Ching*. that later became the foundation for the specialized interpretation of martial arts at Shaolin.

The content of this training has come down to the present time as:

Ye Gun Kung - Exercises designed to strengthen the physical body by working the tendons.
Sai Choi Kung - The art of cleansing (the body - mind) .
Sime Kung - Meditation practice incorporating: stationary or moving exercises training the practitioner to sense, improve and finally control the movement of the Chi in his body; and spiritual training, an effort to directly perceive one's 'Original face' or 'Buddha Nature' .
There are 3 exercises that given to Shaolin monks by Bodhidharma

1) The 18 Luohan Hands
2) Sinew Metamorphosis
3) Bone Marrow Cleansing

Over time, these fighting monks adapted the moves taught by Bodhidharma into early versions of Chinese martial arts techniques that developed through the early history of the Shaolin into rudimentary forms of kung fu.

THE 18 LUOHAN HANDS

There is a famous saying, ***"all martial arts under heaven originated from Shaolin,"*** and all styles at Shaolin originated from Luohan 18 hands and Luohan quan. The word *Luohan* comes from the Sanskrit word *Arhat*. Both words refer to a person who has cultivated a high level of spirituality, After the Buddha passed away, 500 of his top disciples gathered together in a grand council. Together, they reviewed and discussed his teachings word by word. These disciples became known as the 500 Arhats. Bodhidharma, while visiting the Shaolin Temple taught the monks a series of exercises. based on Buddhist teachings, by observing and imitating the forms and expressions of Arhat statues in the temple, meditation and practice, those ancient exercises later evolved into a combat form called "18 hands of Luohan" *luohan shi ba shou*), which is the oldest documented, systematized style of Shaolin Kung Fu. According to the historical official text of Shaolin temple, "Shaolin Kung fu Manual" *shao lin quan pu*), in the Sui dynasty (581-618 AD) Shaolin monks had a selected set of 18 simple movements; until the Tang dynasty (618-907 AD) the set had developed into 18 martial postures, that were combined into a form *tao lu*); the number of the postures increased to 36 until the early Song dynasty (960 AD); and in the Jin-Yuan dynasty (1115-1368 AD) it was developed into 173 movements; finally, in the Ming dynasty the system of the 18 hands of Luohan was completed in 18 forms, each form having 18 postures, making a total of 324 postures.

In Shaolin, this style is called "inborn Luohan's 18 hands" *xian tian luo han shi ba shou*), because it was the style with which Shaolin kung fu was born. Monk Shi Deqian, in his efforts to document Shaolin martial arts collected 8 forms of the 18 hands of Luohan into his "Encyclopedia of Shaolin martial arts". Of these forms, most lineages of Shaolin monks have mostly kept only one form, mostly the first, or the eighth form. Shaolin Luohan's 18 hands movements are simple and straight. The methods are mostly done by the palms of the hands. Fists, hook hands, and other hand gestures and kicks are less used. Luohan's 18 hands are considered the elementary forms in Shaolin kung fu.

There is another Luohan's 18 hands style which is different from the original Shaolin Luohan's 18 hands but is more famous. This Luohan's 18 hands style has 18 different methods, consisted of 6 different methods of fist, 1 method of elbow, 2 methods of palm, 4 methods of leg, and 5 methods of joint locking. Of these 18 methods, a form of 24 movements for attack and defense is developed, which can be performed as a solo form or as a duet form. This style is originally from the Hua quan style of Shandong province and has later been adopted into Shaolin curriculum. Luohan quan is considered a completely pure Buddhist Shaolin style. It is the most famous, and of the most important styles of Shaolin kung fu. Shaolin monks developed Luohan quan as an advanced style based on the 18 hands of Luohan. Luohan quan has been created in the early ages of Shaolin temple, but it was first officially documented by Shaolin monks in the "Shaolin Kung Fu Manual" in the early years of the Song dynasty in 960s AD. This style has two forms called small and big Luohan quan, which are considered the oldest excellent styles of Shaolin temple. There is a famous quote that Shaolin Luohan quan has in total 108 different movements. Small Luohan quan has 27 postures /36 movements and big Luohan quan has about 54 postures /72 movements, so 108 movements in total. Big Luohan quan is itself divided into 3 smaller 18-posture forms. Shi Deyang, 31st generation Shaolin monk talks about 6 forms of big Luohan quan, but most people only know these 3 forms. The first 2 forms/sections of big Luohan quan, which has 36 postures in total, is an ancient form called golden child small Luohan quan (*jin tong xiao luo han quan*). Shaolin small and big Luohan quans are also practiced by the folk people of Dengfeng area around Shaolin in a less Luohan-imitative version,) which drops out or simplifies the Luohan-imitating postures of Shaolin original Luohan quan. Shaolin Luohan quan movements, though simple, are highly advanced and deceptive. Attack and defense are masked by Luohan Buddhist postures and come out from unlikely angles.

During the centuries, Luohan quan was developed. A major contribution was by monk Jue Yuan and two others named Li Sou and Bai Yufeng. Finally, as a result of the developments since the Jin and Yuan dynasties until the middle and late Ming dynasty, a Luohan quan system of 18 forms was created, one form for each one of the famous Luohans, which at those times had increased in number to 18 in Chan Buddhism. In this style, each Luohan form is divided into 3 sections, so it has 54 sections in total. This style is less imitative than small&big Luohan quan style and has given up or, at least, transformed many of the famous Luohan-imitating postures. 18 Luohan quan, though very famous, is rarely known. Even inside Shaolin, only a few people in each generation inherit this style completely. There are different versions of 18 Luohan quan. One version has 18 forms for the 18 Luohans, while there are other versions with 9 long forms which altogether represent 18 Luohan characters. As an estimation of the diversity, just notice that Shaolin monk Shi Degen (1914-1970) taught 3 seemingly different versions to 3 of his disciples, Liu Zhenhai, Shi Yongwen, and Zhu Tianxi.

Because of its long history, there are many versions of the Eighteen Lohan Hands being taught today. Shown below are the Eighteen Lohan Hands taught in Shaolin Wahnam School. The illustrations are reproduced from a manual used more than 10 years ago by my chi kung students. The following exercises are taken from shaolin.org you will get more detailes from the following website : https://shaolin.org/chikung/lohan.html

Lifting the Sky

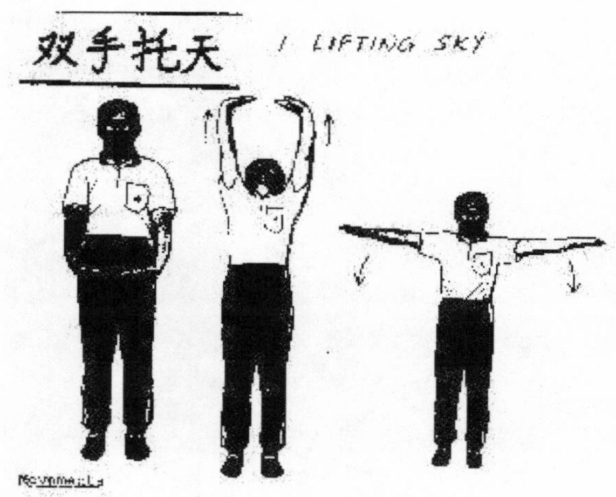

Shooting Arrows

Plucking Stars

Turning Head

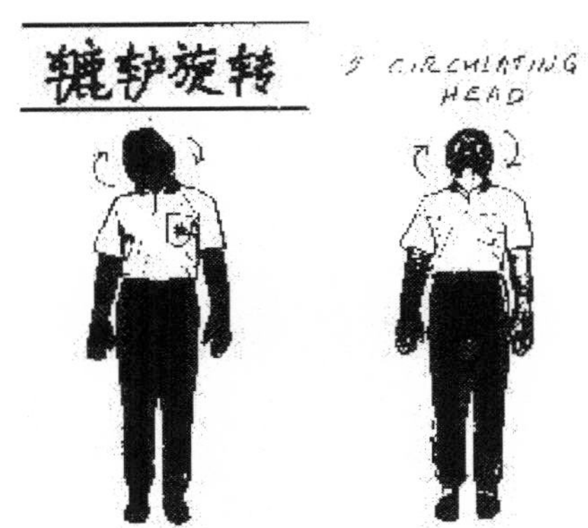

Thrust Punch

Merry-go-Round

Carrying the Moon

Nourishing Kidneys

Three Levels to Ground

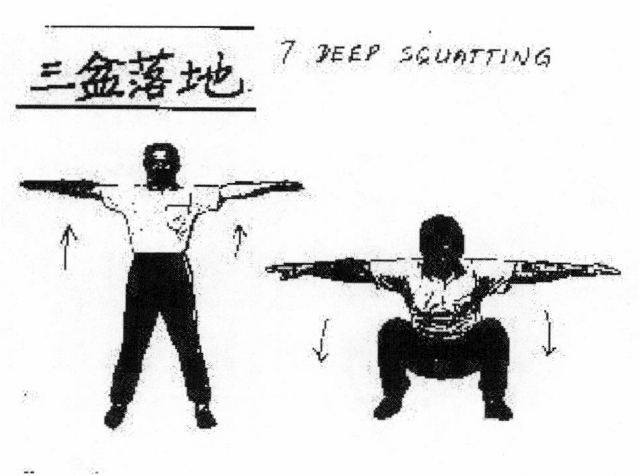

Dancing Crane

Carrying Mountains

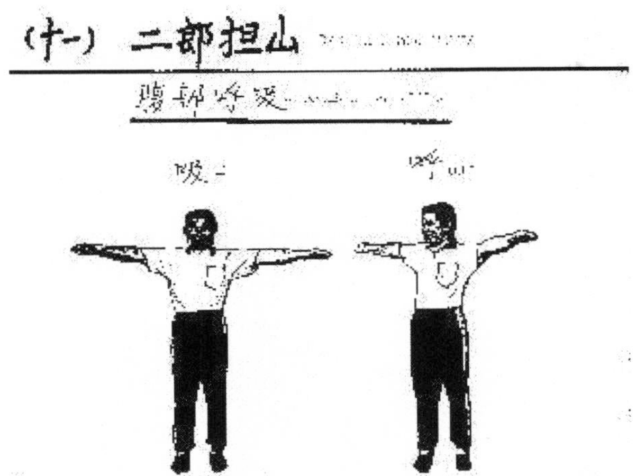

Drawing Knife

Presenting Claws

Pushing Mountains

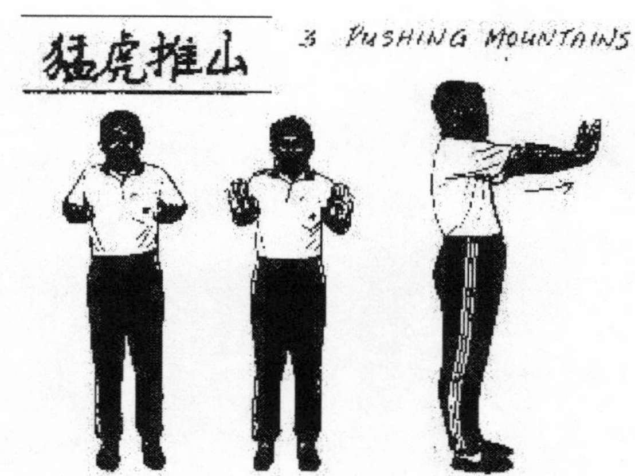

Separating Water

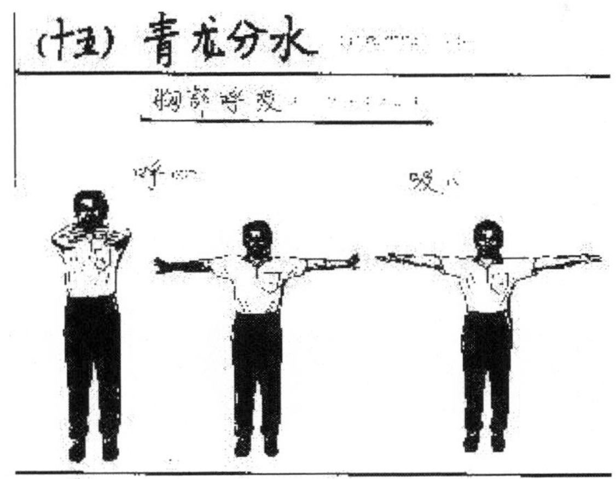

Big Windmill

Deep Knee Bending

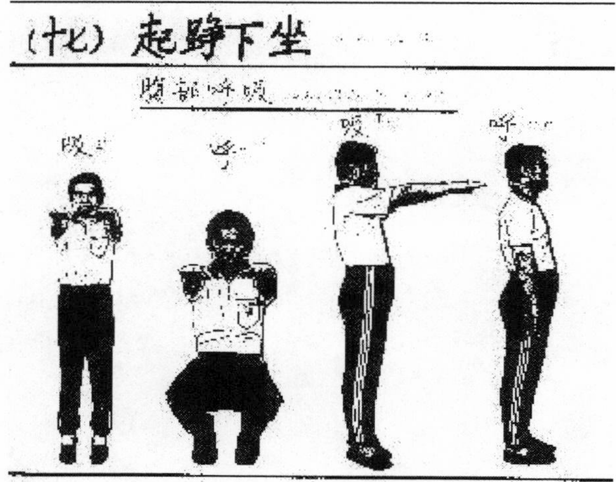

Rotating Knees

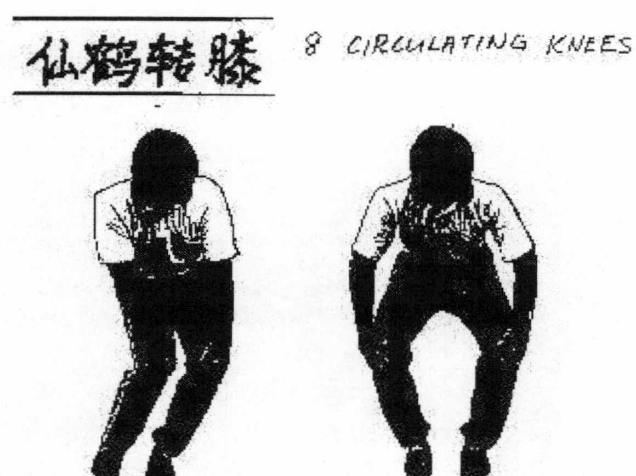

Movements

YIJIN JING (MUSCLE TENDON CHANGING CLASSIC)

The ***Yijin Jing*** is a manual containing a series of exercises, coordinated with breathing, said to enhance physical health dramatically when practiced consistently. It is a mixture of Yoga and Kalaripayattu, an ancient Indian Martial Art from Kalari. Kalaripayattu philosophy is Dharma - Yuddha [War of Truth]. A Dharma - Yuddha begins only if the fighter touches his Masters right hand with his right hand and his opponent chest and hand. This move means that the fight can begin only through the mind and if only heart approved it. Maybe it is not a coincidence that one of the First Shaolin Martial arts named Xin Yi Quan [Heart through mind boxing].

In Chinese yi means "change", jin means "tendons and sinews", while jing means "methods". While some consider these exercises as a form of Qigong, it is a relatively intense form of exercise that aims at strengthening the muscles and tendons, so promoting strength and flexibility, speed and stamina, balance and coordination of the body. In the modern day, there are many translations and distinct sets of exercises all said to be derived from the original (the provenance of which is the subject of some debate). These exercises are notable for being a key element of the physical conditioning used in Shaolin training. The Yijin Jing was said to be left behind by Bodhidharma after his departure from the Shaolin Monastery, and discovered within his grave (or hidden in the walls of the temple) years after he had left. It was accompanied by another text, the *Xisui Jing*, which was passed to a student of Bodhidharma's, but has not survived to the modern day. The monks of Shaolin supposedly practiced the exercises within the text but lost the true purpose of the document; Lin Boyuan recounts the legend that they "selfishly coveted it, practicing the skills therein, falling into heterodox ways, and losing the correct purpose of cultivating the Way" .

Yi Jin Jing is a relatively intense form of exercise that aims at strengthening the muscles and tendons, so promoting strength and flexibility, speed and stamina, balance and coordination of the body.The Yi Jin Jing taught the

Shaolin Monks how to build their internal energy [Qi] to an abundant level and use it to improve health and change their physical bodies from weak to strong. After the Monks practiced the Yi Jin Jing exercises, they found that not only did they improve their health, but also they also greatly increased their strength. When this training was integrated into the martial arts forms, it increased their martial techniques. This change marked one more step in the growth of the Shaolin Martial Arts.The Shaolin monks have made some fame for themselves through their fighting skill; this is all due to having obtained this manuscript. Both documents were written in an Indian language which was not well understood by the monks of the temple. According to one legend, a monk decided that the text must contain more valuable knowledge than simply self-defense, and went on a pilgrimage with a copy of the text to find someone who could translate the deeper meaning of the text. He eventually met an Indian priest named Pramati in the province of Szechwan who, examining the text, explained that the meaning of the text was extraordinarily deep and beyond his ability to translate fully. He nonetheless provided a partial translation. The monk found that within a year of practicing the techniques as Pramati had translated, that his constitution had become "as hard as steel," and he felt that he could be a Buddha. The monk was so pleased that he thereafter followed Pramati wherever he went.

The number of exercises tends to change; some contend that 18 should be the correct one (if based on the 18 Arhats), but can vary from 10 to 24, to 30. Today the most respected routine is that of Wang Zuyuan, composed of 12 exercises, and has been adopted by the Academies of Chinese Medicine in China. Chang Renxia together with Chang Weizhen proposed an alternative set of 14 exercises, which can be of interest for the therapeutic effects he promises. Deng Mingdao presents a version with 24 exercises, but with another name, *Xisui Jing*. In fact, another point of contention is the relationship between the *Xisui Jing* and the *Yijin Jing*. Some authors tend to use those two names for the same routine; others keep things separated and invoke different results and different effects on the body. The 12 Posture Moving Exercise kept to this day is something that Wang Zuyuan learned at the Shaolin Monastery on Mount Song. It is somewhat different from the original "Picture of stationary exercise" and the "Guide to the art of attack" (as Guangdong sources demonstrate). The

12 Posture Moving Exercise supposedly describes what is called the purported "12 fists of Bodhidharma" in many Southern martial arts, most notably Hung Gar and Wing chun. Legend states that the 12 exercises were developed based on the movements of the 12 animals that Bodhidharma studied after his 9 years of meditation. These exercises aided the health of the Shaolin Monastery monks, and contributed to many of the animal-based martial arts in China. The basic purpose of *Yijin Jing* is to turn flaccid and frail sinews and tendons into strong and sturdy ones. The movements of *Yijin Jing* are at once vigorous and gentle. Their performance calls for a unity of will and strength, i.e. using one's will to direct the exertion of muscular strength. It is coordinated with breathing. Better muscles and tendons means better health and shape, more resistance, flexibility, and endurance.

According to an ancient book from Song Dynasty, the spirit can be improved if you practice the method continuously.

- The first year of training gives back physical and mental vitality.
- The second year enhances blood circulation and nurtures meridians.
- The third year allows flexibility to muscles and nurtures the organs.
- The fourth year improves meridians and nurtures viscera.
- The fifth year washes the marrow and nurtures the brain.

The Five rules of *Yijin Jing* are:

- Quietness
  Like lake water reflects the moon, a calm spirit allows energy to move inside the body.
- Slowness
  In order to use and flex muscles deeply, to get maximum extension and move Qi and Xue, slow movements are required.
- Extension
  Each movement must be brought to the maximum.
- Pause
  Efficacy comes through waiting and keeping tension for a longer time.
- Flexibility
  Limbs and trunk must be extended so that blood and energy can circulate, so we have flexibility.

The twelve movements are as follows :

First Movement:

HOLDING BOTH HANDS LIKE ARCHES IN FRONT OF THE CHEST

Second Movement:

HOLDING LOADS WITH BOTH ARMS HORIZONTALLY

Third Movement:

USING PALMS TO SUPPORT THE HEAVEN GATE

Fourth Movement:

GRABBING THE STAR AND CHANGING THE MEASURING EQUIPMENT

Fifth Movement:

TURNING TO GRAB THE NINE OX´S TAIL

Sixth Movement:

PUT OUT TALON AND SHOW THE WING

Seventh Movement:

PULL OUT THE HORSE SABER POSTURE

Eighth Movement:

THREE FALLS TO THE GROUND

Ninth Movement:

GREEN DRAGON REACHES OUT WITH TALONS

Tenth Movement:

HUNGRY TIGER LAUNCHES TO SEIZE THE PREY

Eleventh Movement:

SHOOTING ARROW AND HITTING THE DRUM

Twelfth Movement:

DROP THE TAIL POSTURE

BONE MARROW CLEANSING (XI SUI JING)

Bone Marrow Cleansing (Xi Sui Jing) is the third Chi Kung treasure taught by the Great Bodhidharma in the Shaolin temple. Unlike to the 18 Lohan Hands and the 12 exercises of Sinew Metamorphosis there are no pictures and records on how Bone Marrow Cleansing was practiced in the Shaolin temple. In contrast to the two sets of exercises we interpret Bone Marrow Cleansing as a master' s skill without physical outward form.

Further development in shaolin kung fu

Originally used as exercise, the Kung Fu eventually had to be used against attacking assailants after the monastery's assets. Shaolin eventually became famous for its warrior monks who were masterful in their practice of Kung Fu. Being Buddhist monks, however, they were bound by a set of principles called martial ethics, *wude*, that includes prohibitions such as "do not betray your teacher" and "do not fight for frivolous reasons" as well as eight "hit" and "do not hit" zones to ensure the opponent will not be too seriously injured. As their fighting prowess grew, their skills began to be called upon by leading political figures to take action in times of war.

One famous example of this happened sometime in the 7th century when Emperor T'ai Tsung asked the Shaolin monks to aid him in retrieving his son, who had been kidnapped by his enemy General Wang-Shih-Chung. Legend has it that the temple sent 13 monks, who aided the emperor' s army in defeating the rebellious general and in rescuing his son; as a reward they were given 600 acres of land and their main temple in Henan was given the title *Number One Temple*. Over the years, the monks allied with other leaders involved in conflicts but were not always on the winning side which sometimes led to them seeking refuge in other areas. As they did so, they took their religious and martial arts teaching with them and many other temples became a part of the Shaolin sect, most notably ;

- The Fukien Temple
- The Kwangtung Temple
- The Wu-Tang Temple
- The O Mei Shan Temple

The temples were, in many regards, like universities and students would have to learn many subjects in order to graduate such as religion, philosophy, medicine and of course martial arts. Many different styles of fighting have evolved in China and exactly how this happened was often dependent on geological factors. In the South it is often wet and muddy which has given over to greater emphasis on hand to hand combat and in crowded areas such as the sea ports, grappling techniques are more common. In the north, it is dryer and tends to be more open so longer range techniques such as jumping kicks prospered, though this is very general and there is a large amount of overlap.

At the beginning of the 10th century, the history of Shaolin kung fu saw important developments when a young monk by the name of Chueh Yuan reformed the martial arts being practiced there when he created *the 72 Movements*. They focused on both internal and external fitness and once devised, Chueh Yuan began a journey to teach his new style and to learn from others. While on his travels, Chueh Yuan met a master named Pai Yu-Feng who was knowledgeable in the body' s pressure points; the two teamed up and combined their knowledge to create 170 exercises that became the basis of modern Shaolin kung fu. This also began a tradition of monks leaving the temple to learn from outsiders once they attained a certain level of mastery in the martial arts. This was done so that they could bring back new skills and teachings when they returned to the temple to which they belonged. In 1417, a monk connected to the Wu-Tang temple by the name of Chang Sanfeng is believed by some to have developed a style that was more reminiscent of the Taoist philosophies of a bygone era. It focused on internal energy and harmony and was inspired, so the legend goes, when he watched a fight between a snake and a bird. It is hard to know how much of this story is true and how much fabricated later but it seems a system was developed at the time that would evolve into modern day Tai Chi Chuan (Mind Fist).

Another major development that came out of the Shaolin Temple happened in the 16th century when Zhue Yuen, Li Sou and Bai Yu Feng developed the *Five Animal Styles*. These new systems combined the hard and soft aspects of Chinese martial arts and were not only fighting techniques, but showed ways to handle situations in everyday life.They were devised to represent different aspects of human development through metaphor, they were;

- Tiger – To developed tough bones
- Leopard – To build strength
- Snake – To develop internal energy (chi)
- Dragon – To cultivate spirit
- Crane – To strengthen the sinews

The End of an Era

Shaolin kung fu styles continued to develop and be handed down from one generation of monks to the next until in 1644, China saw a regime change. After almost 300 years of rule, the Ming Dynasty was overthrown by the Ching (Qing) Dynasty, who did not favour the monks of the Shaolin or their teachings. A short time later, they destroyed the temple in the Henan Province killing most of the monks in the process, however a few grandmasters did survive. They went into hiding and some found students to pass on their kung fu knowledge to.

FEW LAST THOUGHTS

Through this book, i am tried to paint a picture of the life and teachings of Bodhidharma, and thus bring some light into the enigmatic accounts of Bodhidharma. The Buddha showed a path beyond religion that showed the original simplicity and perfection of mind. In spite of that, due to the general habits of humanity, religiosity creeped into even various Buddhist systems from time to time. However, the open culture of Buddhism paved way for many visionary masters who could again step beyond such religiosity and bring the focus back to the essence of realizing one' s own nature. Bodhidharma was such a revolutionary master who dispelled religiosity and drove disciples straight into the essence of Buddhism. As an example of how every walk of life can be turned into a Way of Bodhi (awakening), he showed how even martial arts can be turned into a meaningful and peaceful activity, a wild leap of awakening.

Manufactured by Amazon.ca
Bolton, ON